Easy Peasy
All-in-One Homeschool

Preschool
Workbook

To be used ALONG WITH the online course

2018 Edition

All-in-One
Homeschool

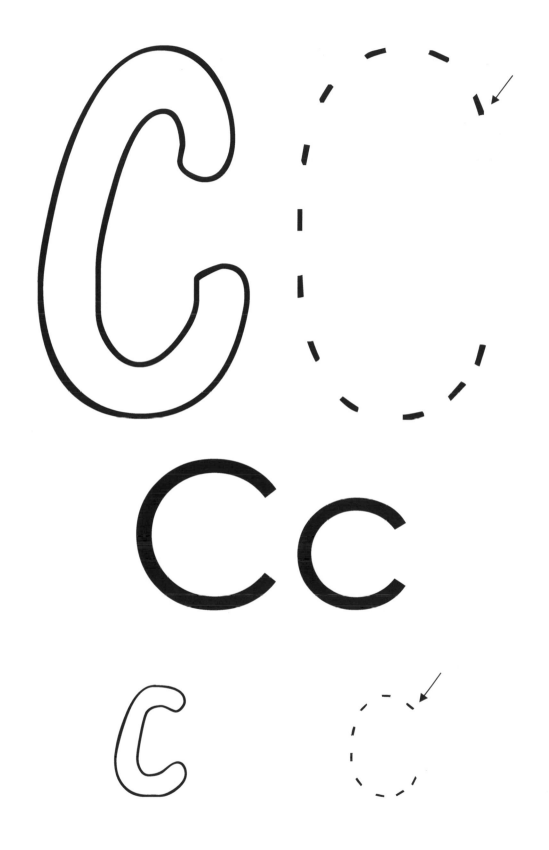

Circle

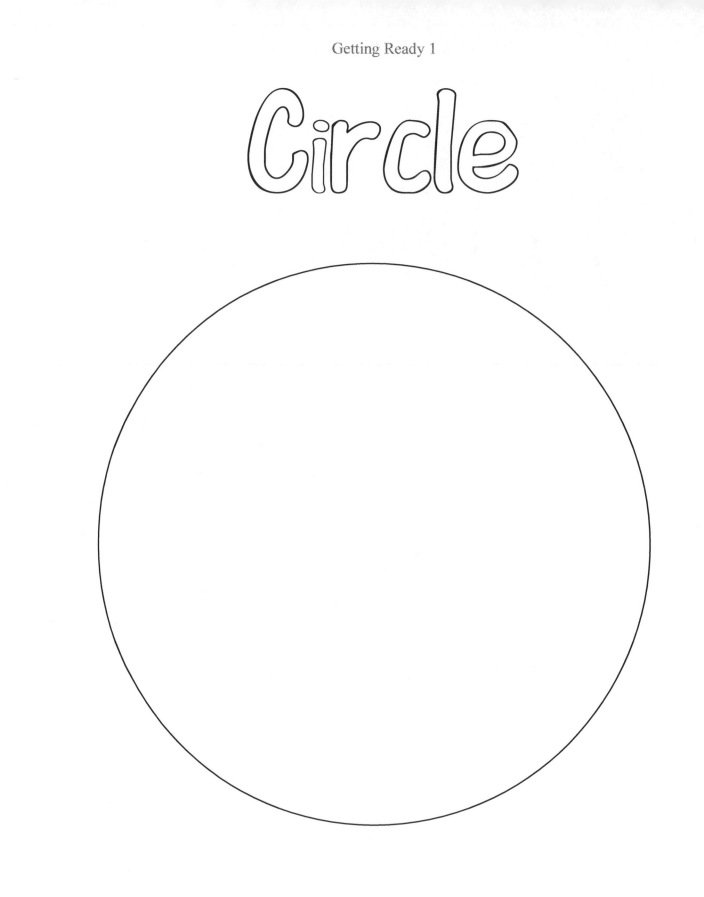

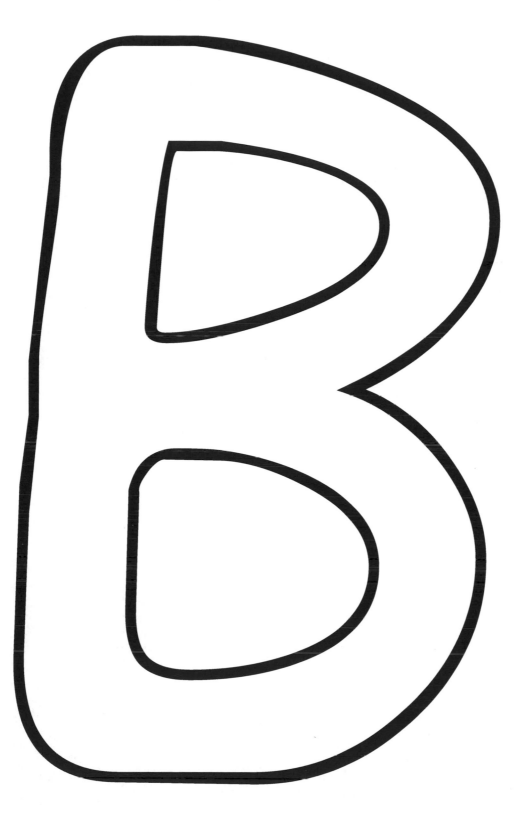

C c

Find the letters.

Caribou are also known as reindeer. They are found in the Arctic where it is very cold. Can you see what's on its head?

Dd

Danielle the Dog

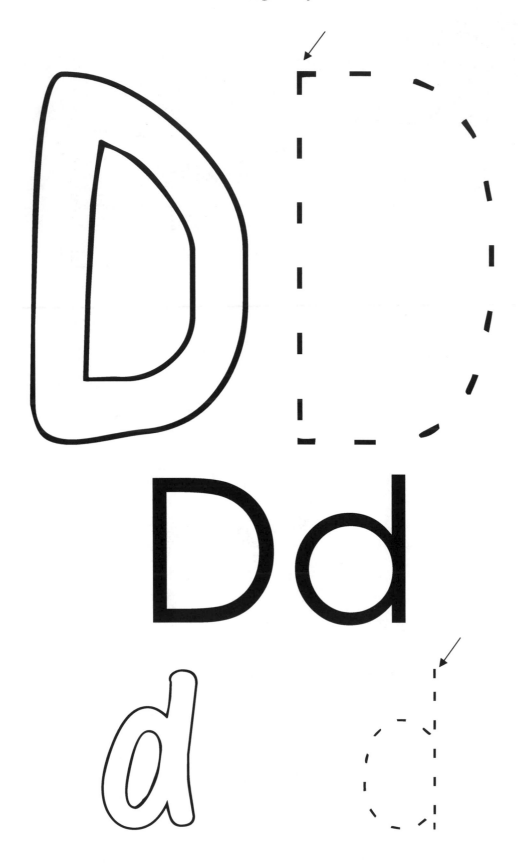

D d

Find the letters.

Dolphins live in the ocean. They have curved mouths that make them look friendly. They can be trained to do tricks.

Ee

Elizabeth the Elephant

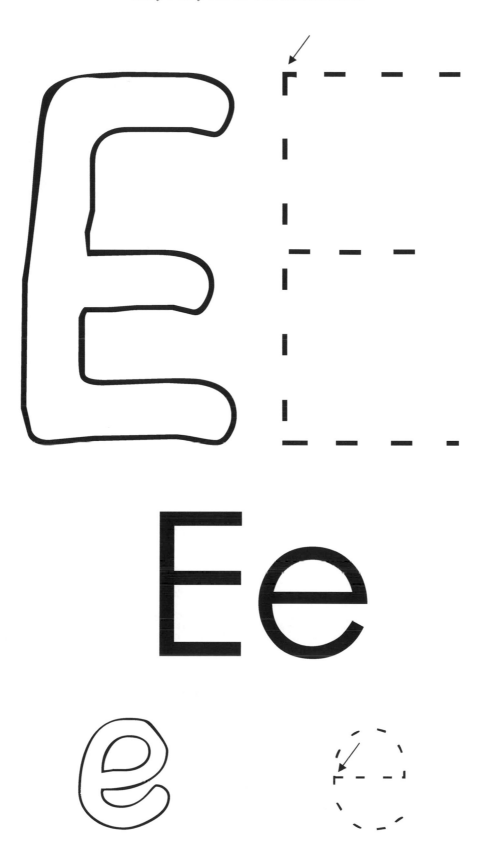

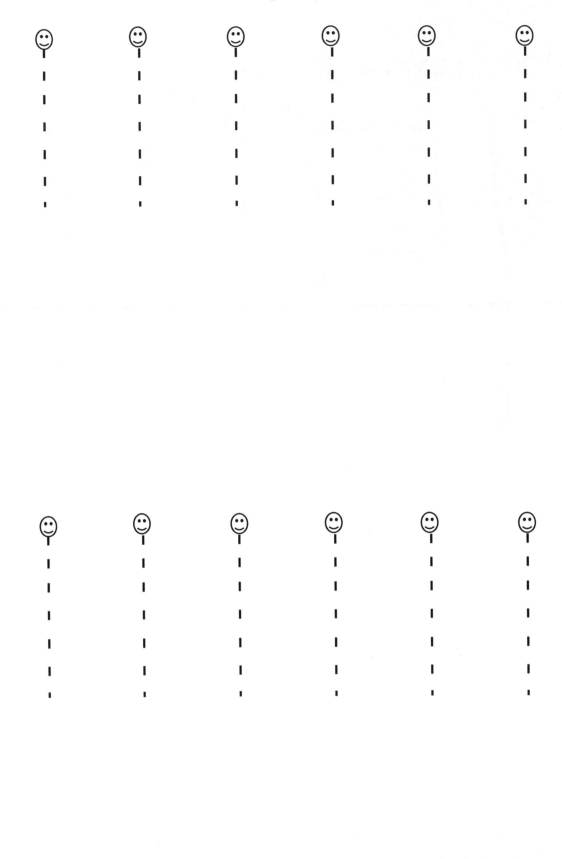

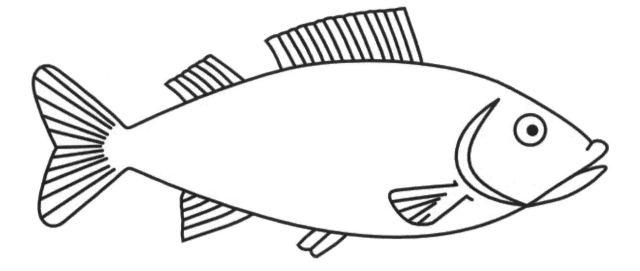

F f

Faith
the
Fish

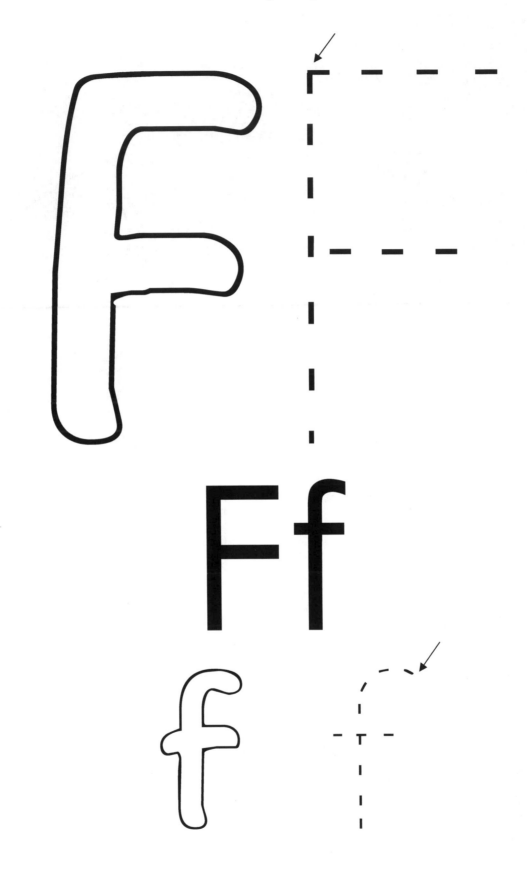

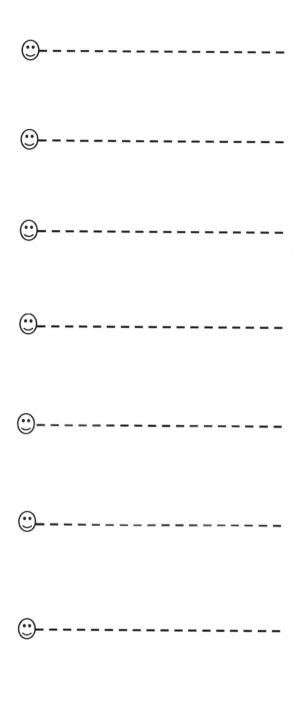

F f

Find the letters.

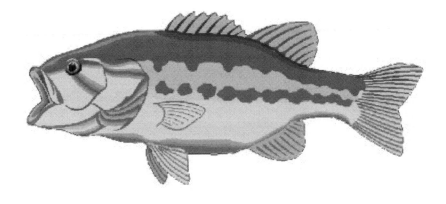

Fish come in many shapes and sizes. They swim free in oceans, seas, lakes, and rivers. Have you ever gone fishing? Do you eat fried fish?

E e

Find the letters.

African elephants are the largest land animals on Earth. They have bigger ears than Asian elephants.

G g g

Greg
the
Goat

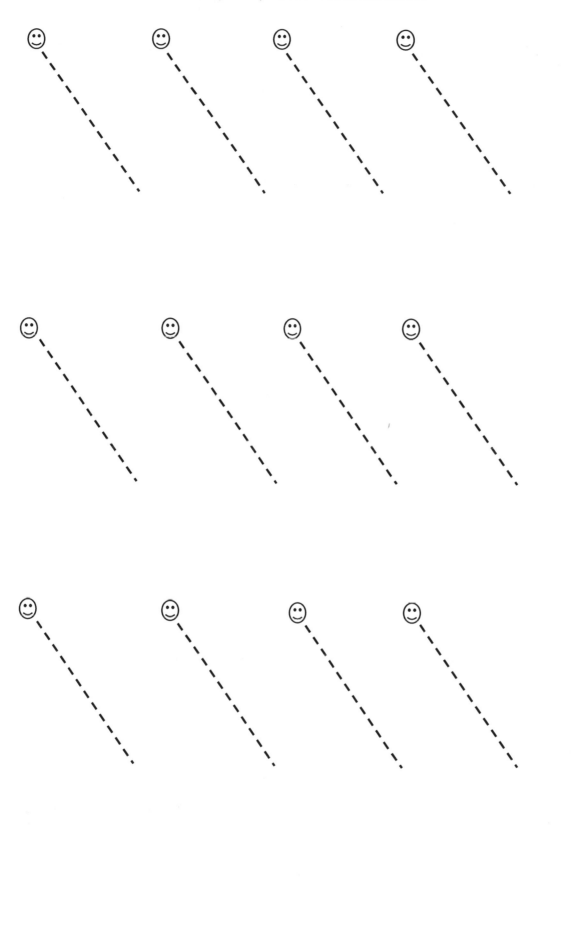

G g

Find the letters.

Gazelles live in the grasslands. They live in groups and can move very fast. Gazelles have hooves on their feet.

28

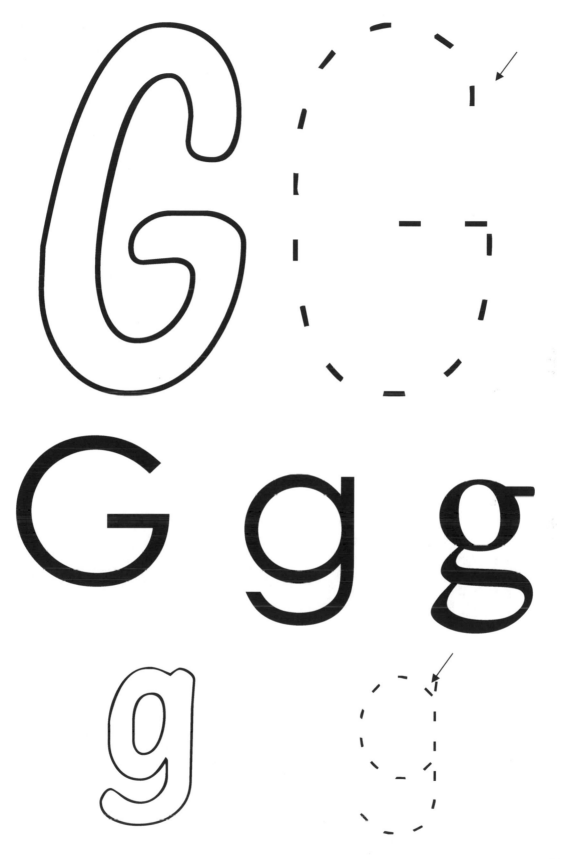

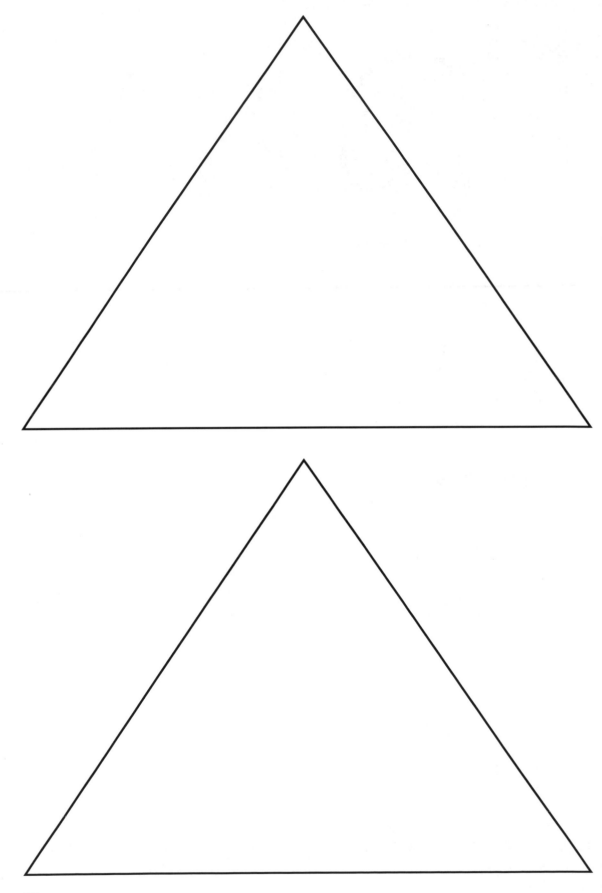

Hh

Harold
the
Hippo

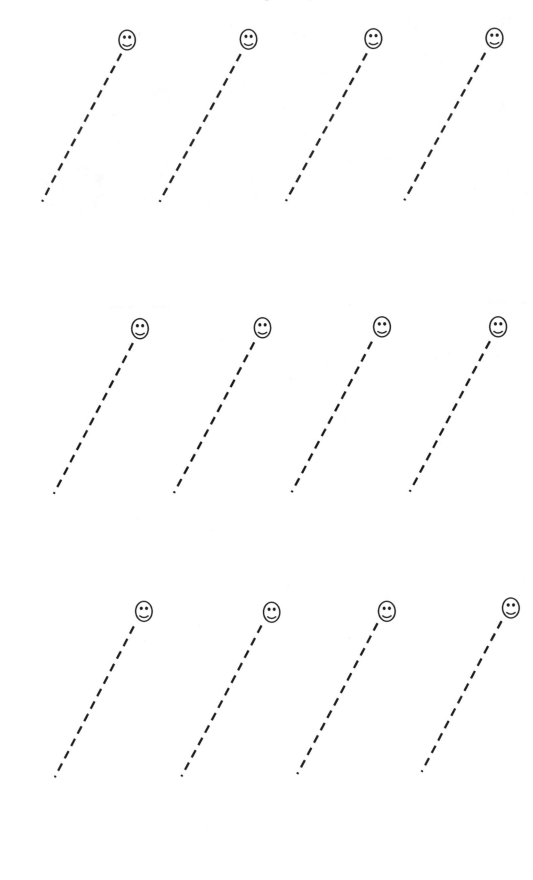

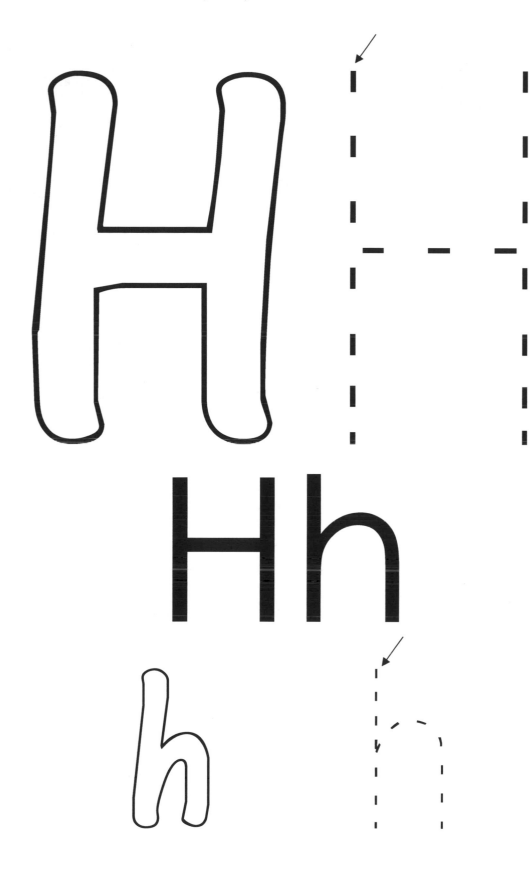

Ii

Isaac
the
Iguana

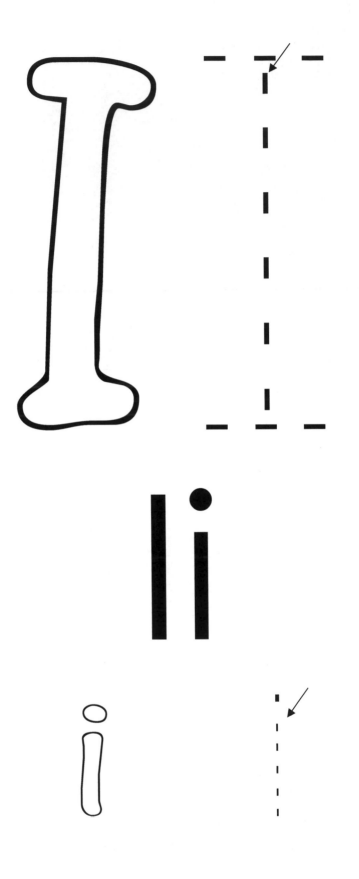

I i

Find the letters.

Iguanas are a type of lizard.

Green iguanas live in the rain

forest and eat leaves and fruit.

They are excellent swimmers.

Connect the dots in the order of the alphabet.

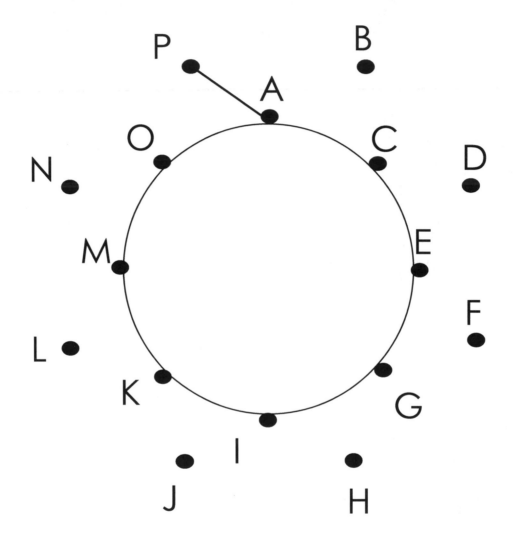

H h

Find the letters.

Horses live in North America as well as in other continents. The hair on the back of their head is called a mane.

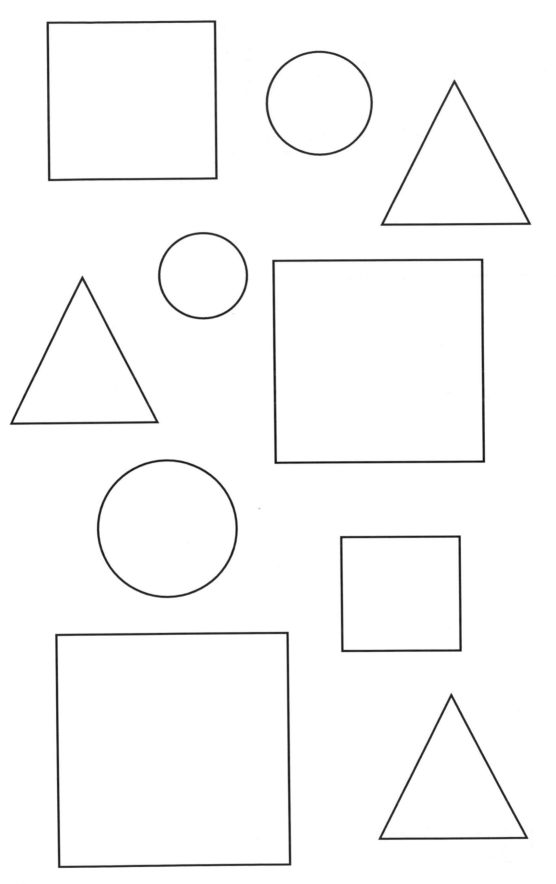

Jj

John
the
Jaguar

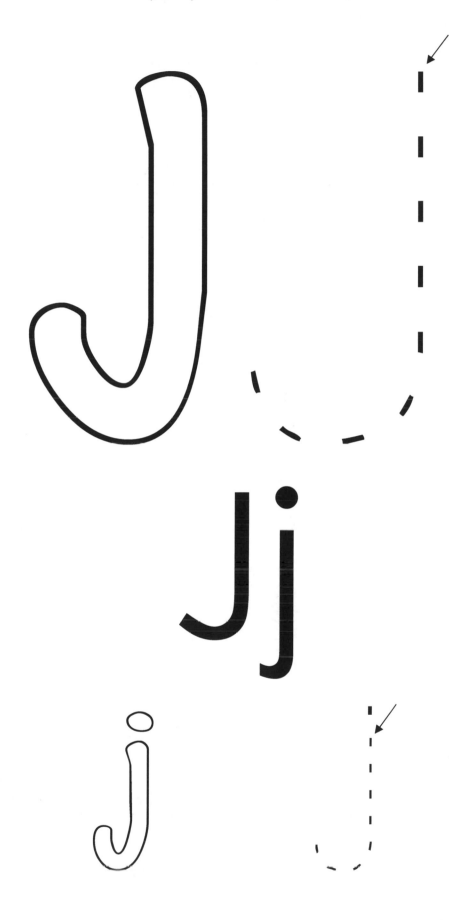

J j

Find the letters.

Jellyfish live in the ocean. They journey along ocean currents. Some jellyfish use jets to move themselves in the water.

Kk

Keith
the
Kangaroo

K

Kk

k

Ll

Lee
the
Lion

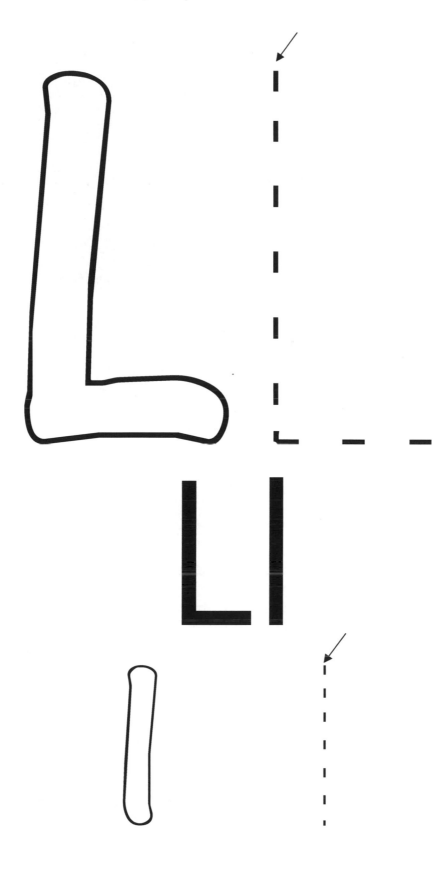

L l

Find the letters.

Llamas live in South America. They are used by people to carry loads. Llamas eat plants and don't need a lot of water.

51

K k

Find the letters.

Koalas live in Australia. Koalas snack on eucalyptus leaves which are poisonous, but koalas have a trick to eating them.

Mm

Michelle
the
Monkey

M M

Mm

m m

M m

Find the letters.

Manatees live in the ocean. They are slow swimmers. They move around in small groups. Manatees are mammals.

Nn

Nicole the Nuthatch

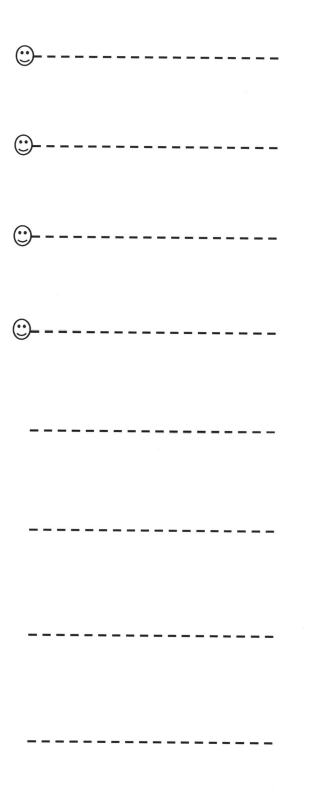

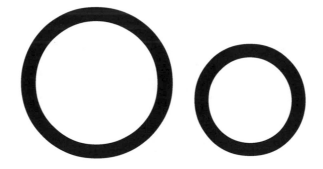

Olivia the Octopus

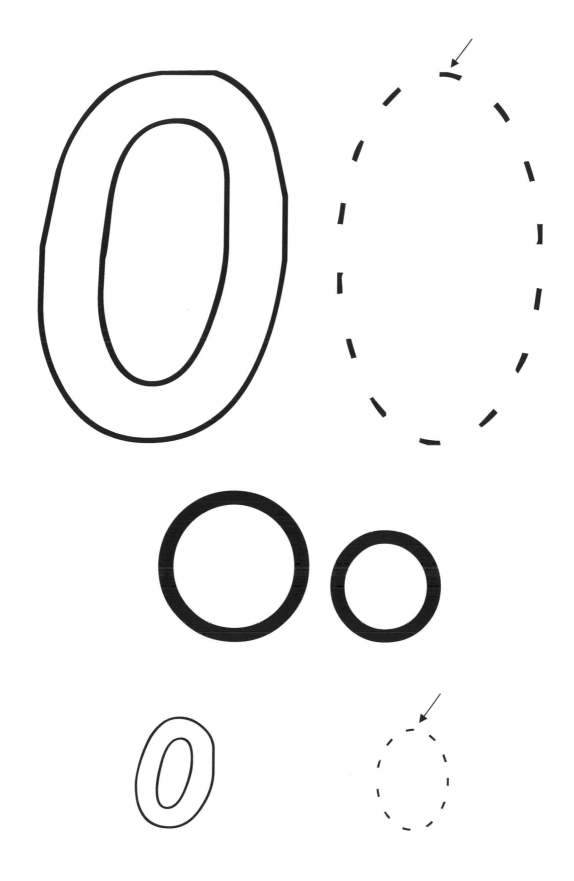

O o

Find the letters.

Giant river otters can be six feet long. They live in the Amazon. Mostly they eat fish for their food. Otters are mammals.

N n

Find the letters.

Narwhals are interesting ocean animals. They have two teeth. One grows into a tusk, a pointy sword coming from its mouth.

Pp

Paul
the
Parrot

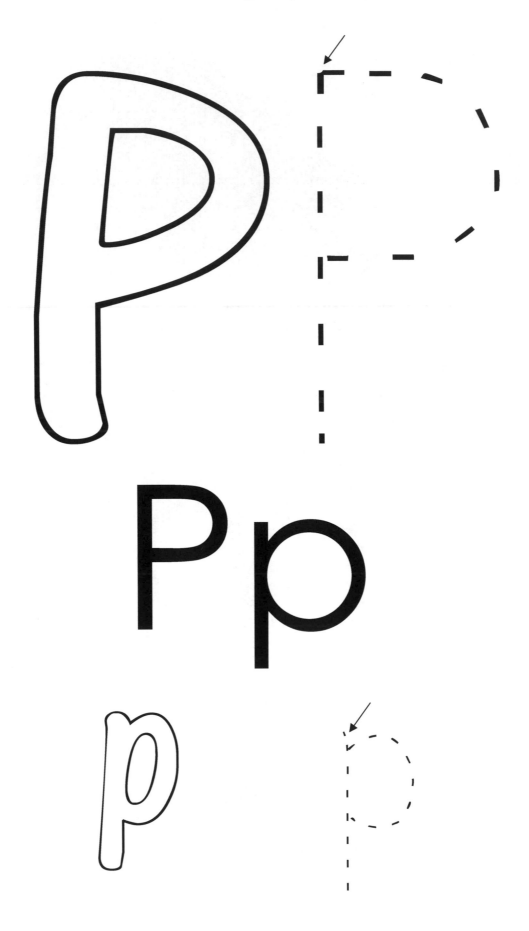

P p
Find the letters.

Giant pandas' place is in China. People pick them out by their color, but they are born white. Pandas pick bamboo to eat.

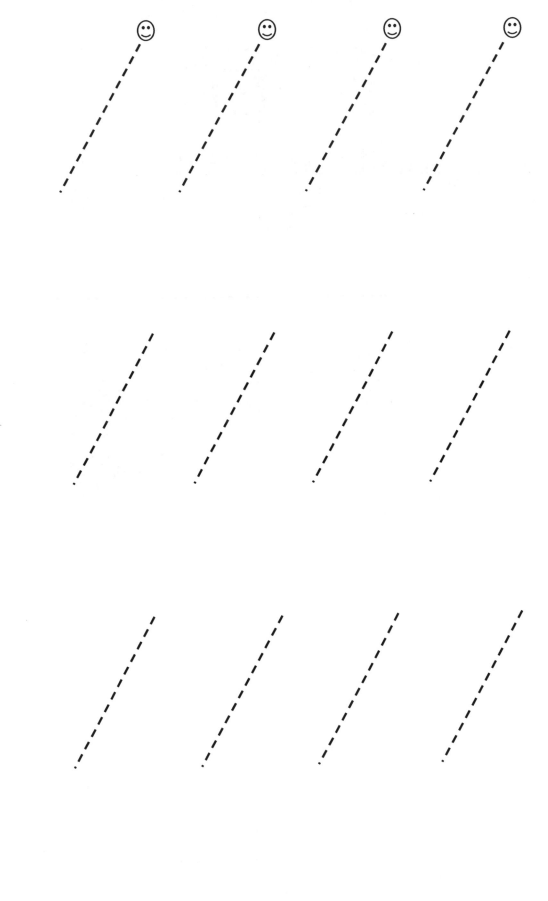

Qq

Queenie
the
Queen Bee

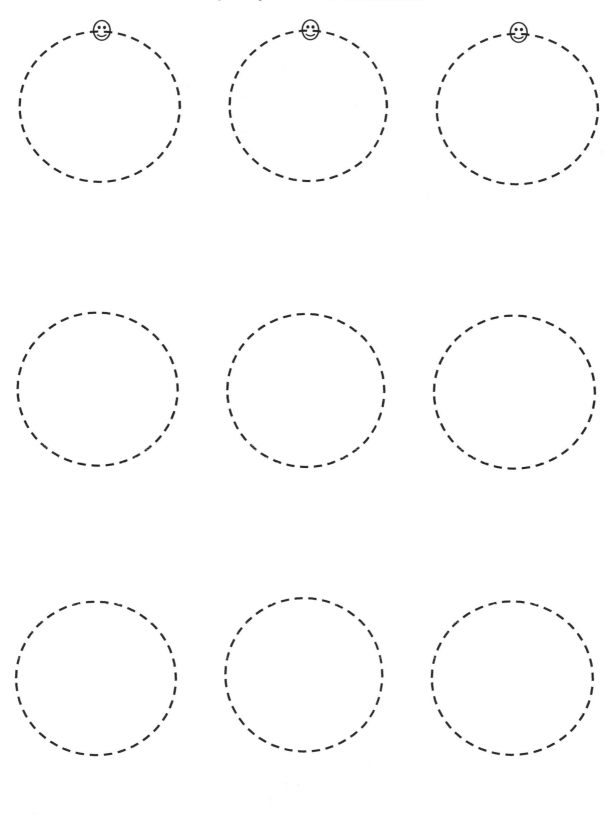

Rr

Robert
the
Rabbit

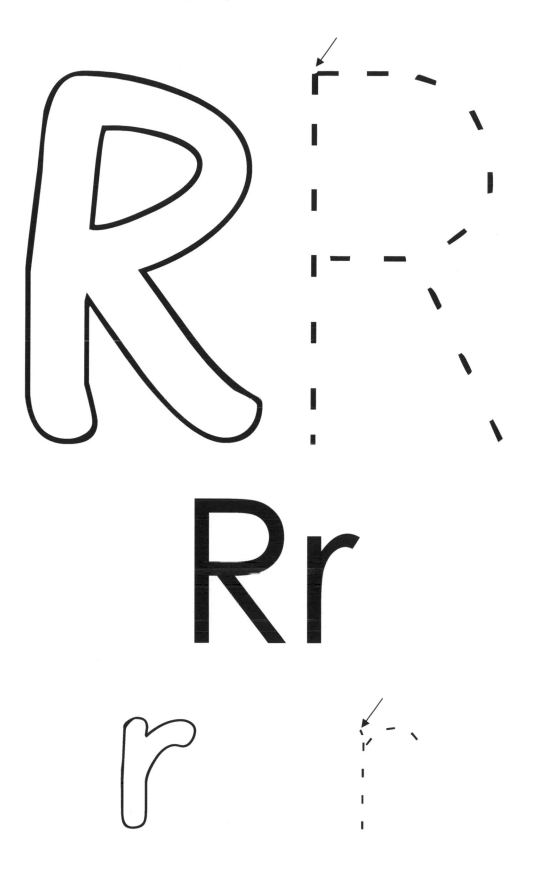

R r

Find the letters.

Racoons live all over, and they eat almost anything. After dark they use their front paws to grab the food they find.

Q q

Find the letters.

One type of quail lives a quiet life in California. The male can be quite beautiful with a feather plume on his head.

Ss

Sammy
the
Snake

S s

Find the letters.

Skunks live in North America. They are known for their smell which they shoot in defense. The scent is strong and awful.

Tt

Timothy
the
Turtle

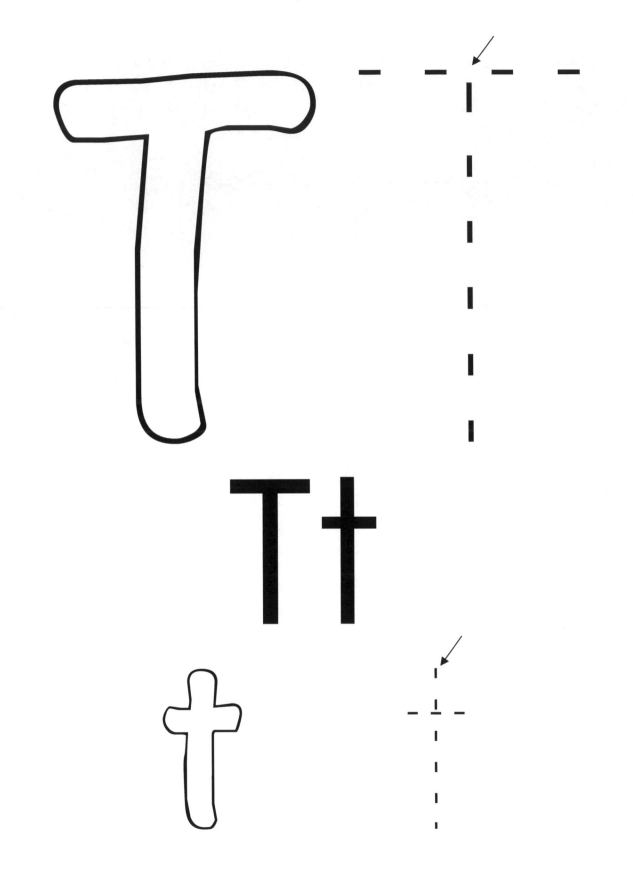

Uu

Ulysses the Unicorn

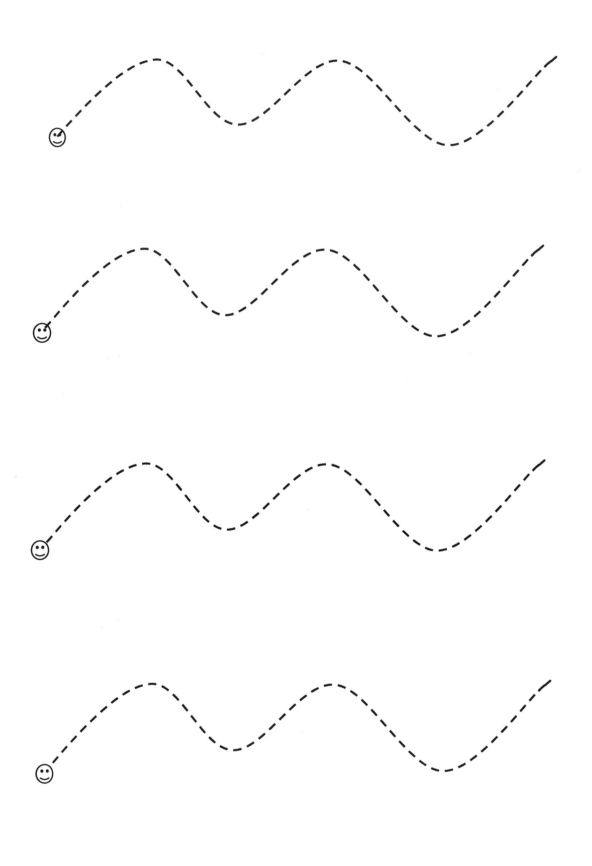

U u
Find the letters.

Some squirrels live up in trees, and some squirrels live under ground. They have four front teeth. They like to eat nuts.

T t

Find the letters.

Tigers live in Asia. They are the largest kind of cat. They are targets for hunters. Tigers have a lot of strength.

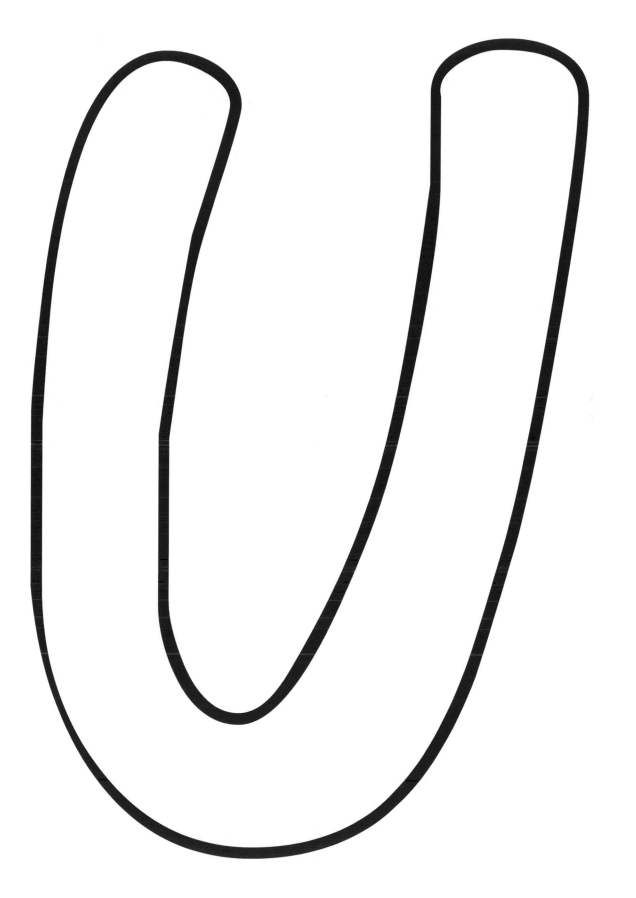

Vv

Victor
the
Vulture

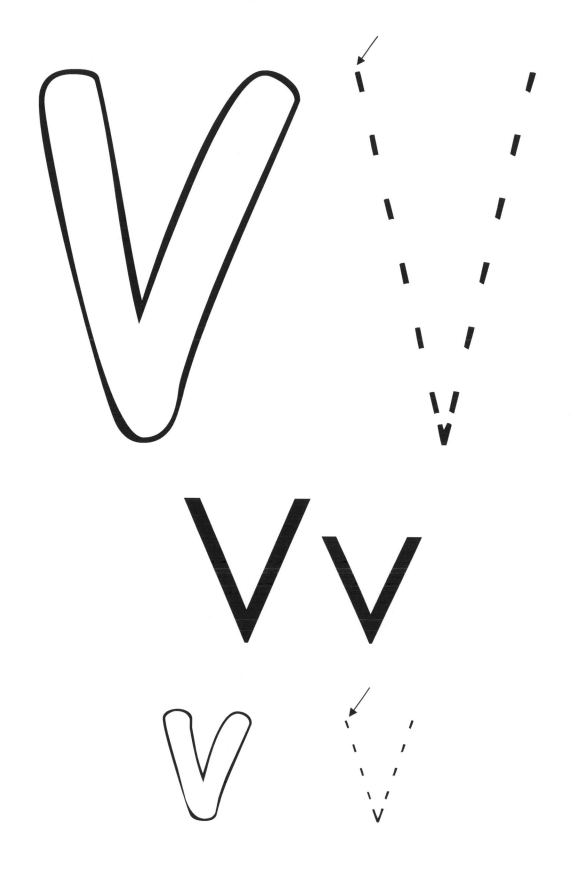

V v

Find the letters.

Wolves live in the Northern Hemisphere, but there are areas in which they have not survived because they are killed.

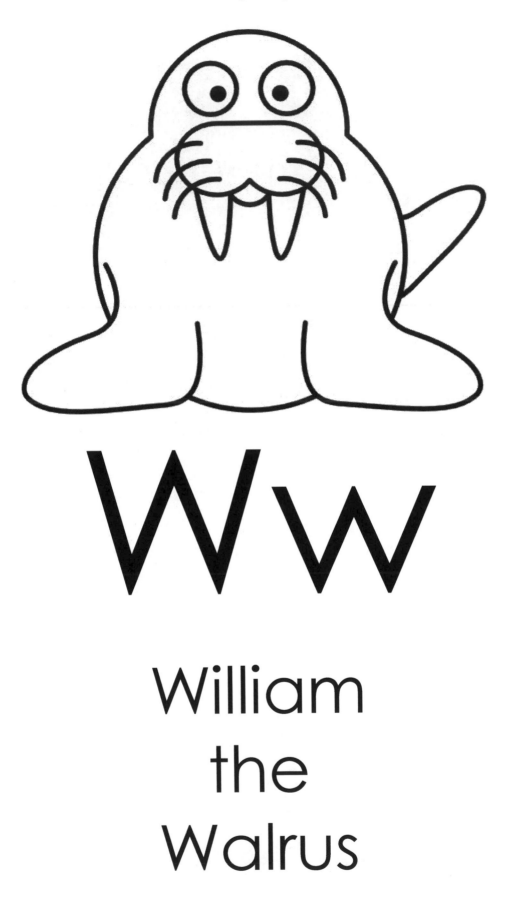

Ww

William
the
Walrus

Xx

Xavier
the
X-ray Fish

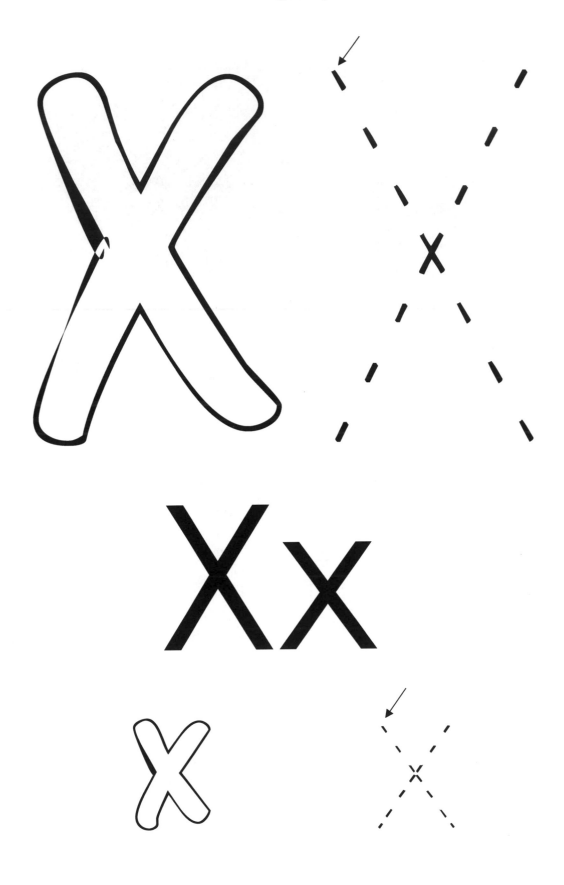

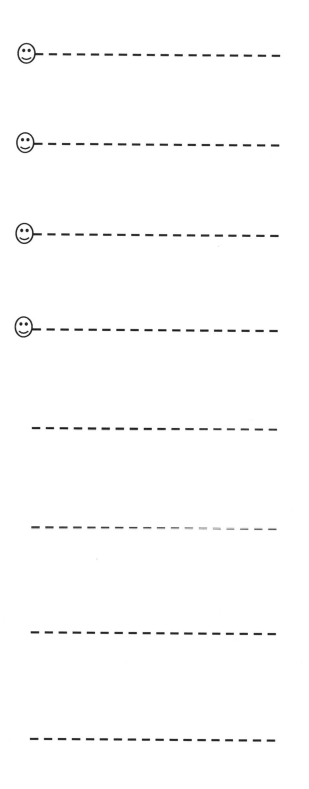

X x

Find the letters.

The lynx live in northern forests. They have extra thick fur coats to keep them warm. Some lynx are in danger of going extinct.

W w

Find the letters.

Blue whales live underwater.

They weigh as much as 100 cars.

In one day they can swallow

about two cars' worth of krill.

Their underside is white.

Yy

Yolanda the Yak

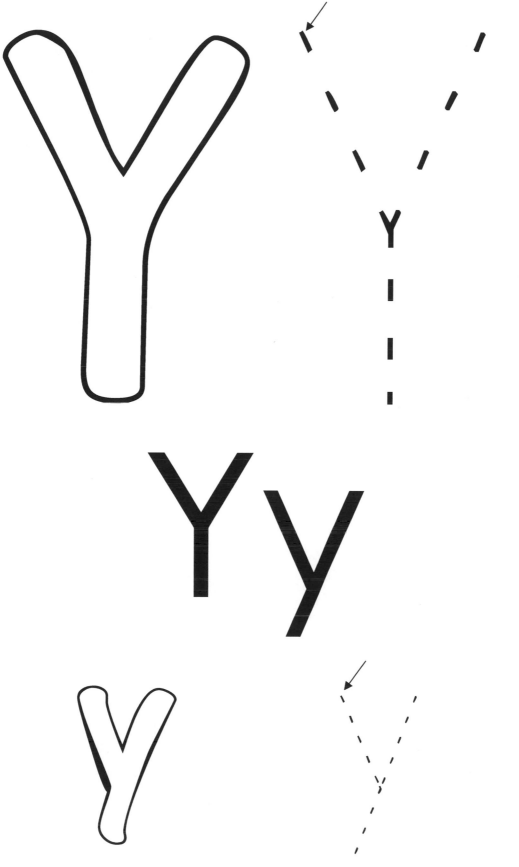

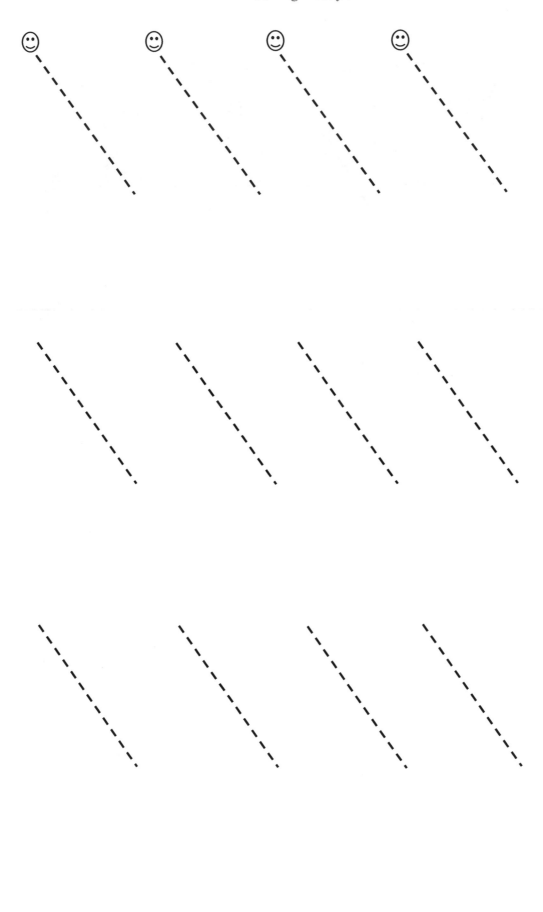

Y y

Find the letters.

The platypus is an interesting animal. They swim gracefully, but walk awkwardly on land. They lay eggs on land.

Zz

Zoe
the
Zebra

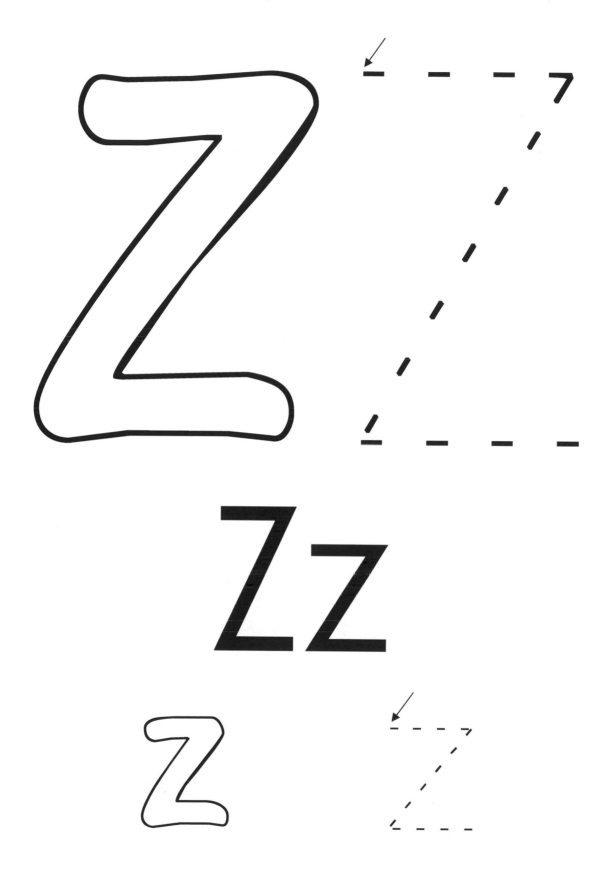

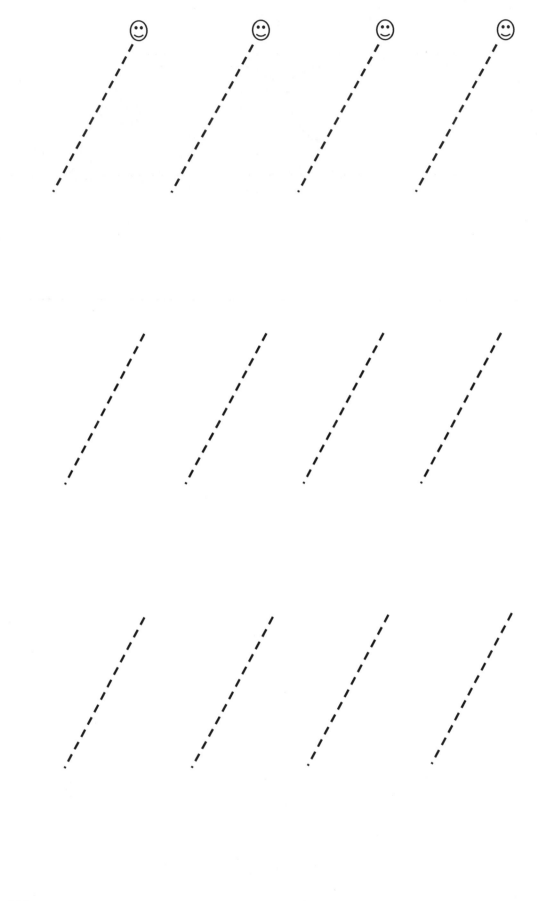

Z z

Find the letters.

Zebras live in Africa. They graze on grass. Each zebra has its own pattern of crazy stripes that confuse its enemies.

I hope you are enjoying learning with Easy Peasy All-in-One Homeschool. Once your child knows the alphabet letters and sounds, it's time to move onto the McGuffey Primer. If you'd like to work offline, consider getting our Learn to Read book which contains the sight words and reading lessons from the Primer.

Made in the USA
Middletown, DE
18 November 2019